Welcome!

From her early days as a Disney star in *Wizards of Waverly Place* to becoming a billionaire beauty mogul, Selena Gomez has left an indelible mark on the entertainment industry. She's an accomplished actress, singer, and producer who has won several awards, broken various records and amassed a huge social media following. But that's not all - she's also a passionate advocate for social causes and uses her platform to raise awareness about important issues that are close to her heart. So, join us as we dive into Selena's incredible life and career with this Ultimate Fan's Guide, featuring four amazing pull-out posters.

Head to the middle of the mag (p55-62) for your **PULL-OUT POSTERS**

ULTIMATE FAN'S GUIDE TO *Selena Gomez*

Early childhood

Born on 22 July 1992 in Grand Prairie, Texas, Selena Marie Gomez was the first child of parents Mandy Teefey and Ricardo Gomez. At the time of her birth, Selena's mother was only 16 years old. Fittingly for her future career, Selena was named after the singer Selena Quintanilla-Perez. As her parents were so young when she was born, much of Selena's early childhood was spent with her grandparents who cared for her while her parents finished school. When Selena was five years old, her parents divorced and from then on she lived with her mother. Before she shot to stardom, Selena and her mother experienced financial difficulties.

ULTIMATE FAN'S GUIDE TO *Selena Gomez*

First acting roles

Selena got her first acting role in 2002 when she played Gianna in the popular children's show *Barney & Friends*. The show revolved around Barney the big purple dinosaur, and in each episode, Barney, friends and the children in the show would learn about a different topic. Selena remained as a recurring character in *Barney & Friends*, acting alongside another future Disney star, Demi Lovato, for two years. After this, Selena auditioned for various other roles, landing a part in the movie *Spy Kids 3-D: Game Over* in 2003, and a smaller part in *Walker, Texas Ranger: Trial by Fire* in 2005. These roles, although minor, gave the young Selena valuable exposure and experience.

ULTIMATE FAN'S GUIDE TO *Selena Gomez*

Beginnings of a Disney star

After playing several smaller parts, Selena was given a minor role in Disney Channel's hugely popular children's show, *The Suite Life of Zack and Cody*, in 2006. Her character, Gwen, only appeared in one episode. However, the part meant that she was now on Disney's radar and in 2007, she got the role of a new recurring character in the series *Hannah Montana*, a show about a teenage girl living a secret life as a pop star. In the show, Selena played Mikayla, another pop star and Hannah Montana's nemesis. She also recorded two pilots for Disney Channel before she won the role that would make her name.

Magical star quality

In 2007, Selena appeared on our screens starring in *Wizards of Waverly Place*, where she became a Disney star. She was 15 when she began her leading role as Alex Russo, a teenage wizard who, alongside her brothers Justin (David Henrie) and Max (Jake T Austin), learns to train her magical abilities – and work in the family sandwich shop! As well as starring in the show, Selena sang the opening song 'Everything Is Not As It Seems', which sums up the show's themes of secret identities perfectly. As much as the series was about the extraordinary, the central family felt wholesome and relatable.

ULTIMATE FAN'S GUIDE TO *Selena Gomez*

Rebooting her cinematic career

Five years after her first foray into the world of cinema, 2008 saw Selena star as the lead, Mary Santiago, in teen musical comedy *Another Cinderella Story* and as Helga McDodd, the daughter of Mayor Ned McDodd (played by Steve Carell), in the animated children's story *Horton Hears a Who!*. *Another Cinderella Story* included a fun pop soundtrack with Selena's vocals taking centre stage but the film was released straight to video with middling reviews and concerns over the age difference between Selena, who was 15 at the time, and the 26-year-old Drew Seeley, who played her love interest Joey. In contrast, *Horton Hears a Who!* was a box-office hit, grossing almost $300 million against an $85 million budget.

'Burnin' Up'

The year 2008 continued to be a very important one for Selena, as she began dating fellow Disney Channel star and singer Nick Jonas. That same year, Selena appeared in a music video for his band, the Jonas Brothers' song 'Burnin' Up'. Although their romance was short-lived, it was anything but forgettable: despite their best efforts to keep it under wraps, the fact that they dated soon after Nick split from *Hannah Montana's* Miley Cyrus caused a social media feud, with Miley and Mandy Jiroux posting a video on YouTube seemingly mocking Selena and her friend, Demi Lovato. Years later, Selena confirmed it had all just been a misunderstanding, adding "we are now completely settled in our own lives".

ULTIMATE FAN'S GUIDE TO *Selena Gomez*

Princess Protection Program

Selena's Disney Channel success continued, when she starred as her *Wizards of Waverly Place* character, Alex Russo, in an episode of *The Suite Life on Deck*, which was a multi-episode crossover event, including characters from *Hannah Montana* as well. In 2009, she also appeared as herself on *Sonny with a Chance*, opposite Demi Lovato. In the previous month, she and Demi led the cast for the Disney Channel movie, *Princess Protection Program*, which won the 2009 Teen Choice Awards for Choice Summer TV Show. Selena and Demi recorded the track 'One And The Same' for the film, which peaked at number 82 on the US Billboard Hot 100.

Wizards of Waverly Place: The Movie

After two successful seasons of *Wizards of Waverly Place*, Disney Channel released a film based on the hit series. Featuring the same cast, the film follows Selena's Alex Russo as she tries to solve a crisis she causes when she wishes her parents had never met after they ground her. The film was wildly popular: it premiered to 11.4 million views and became the second-most-watched Disney Channel Original Movie premiere after *High School Musical 2*. The film won Outstanding Children's Program at the 62nd Primetime Emmy Awards in 2010 and Selena, along with David Henrie and Jake T Austin, who played her brothers, garnered critical praise for their performances.

ULTIMATE FAN'S GUIDE TO *Selena Gomez*

Becoming a UNICEF ambassador

Following on from her work as UNICEF's spokesperson for their Trick-or-Treat campaign, Selena was named the youngest UNICEF ambassador in 2009 when she was just 17 years old. Selena's first official field mission saw her travel to Ghana in September 2009 to witness the impact of the lack of access to clean water, food, education and healthcare for some of the children living there. She told reporters that she felt "very honoured to have a voice that kids listen to and take into consideration". Since then, Selena has raised millions of dollars for the charity, participating in celebrity auctions, holding benefit concerts and embarking on further field missions. In June 2021, she, alongside other UNICEF ambassadors, urged the G7 to improve global access to the coronavirus vaccine.

Launching her music career

At the age of just 16, Selena signed a record deal with Hollywood Records, launching her pop music career and following in the footsteps of fellow Disney Channel star, Miley Cyrus. She also formed her band, Selena Gomez & The Scene, their name derived from common public insults thrown at Selena, which described her as a "wannabe scene". The band released their debut studio album, *Kiss & Tell*, in September 2009 and embarked on a small tour to support the album, playing venues in the US and the UK. The album debuted at number nine on the US Billboard 200, and its second single, 'Naturally', peaked at number seven in the UK.

A Year Without Rain

A year after their debut, Selena Gomez & The Scene released their second studio album, *A Year Without Rain*, to mixed reviews, with many critics calling the album an evolution from *Kiss & Tell* and *Portrait* magazine calling it a "definite improvement". *A Year Without Rain* debuted in the US charts at number four, with hit singles 'Round & Round' and 'A Year Without Rain'. It also featured work by major industry names such as RedOne and Katy Perry and was certified gold in the US, Canada, Brazil and Portugal. The band played 19 shows in venues across Europe, North America and Latin America on their tour to support the album.

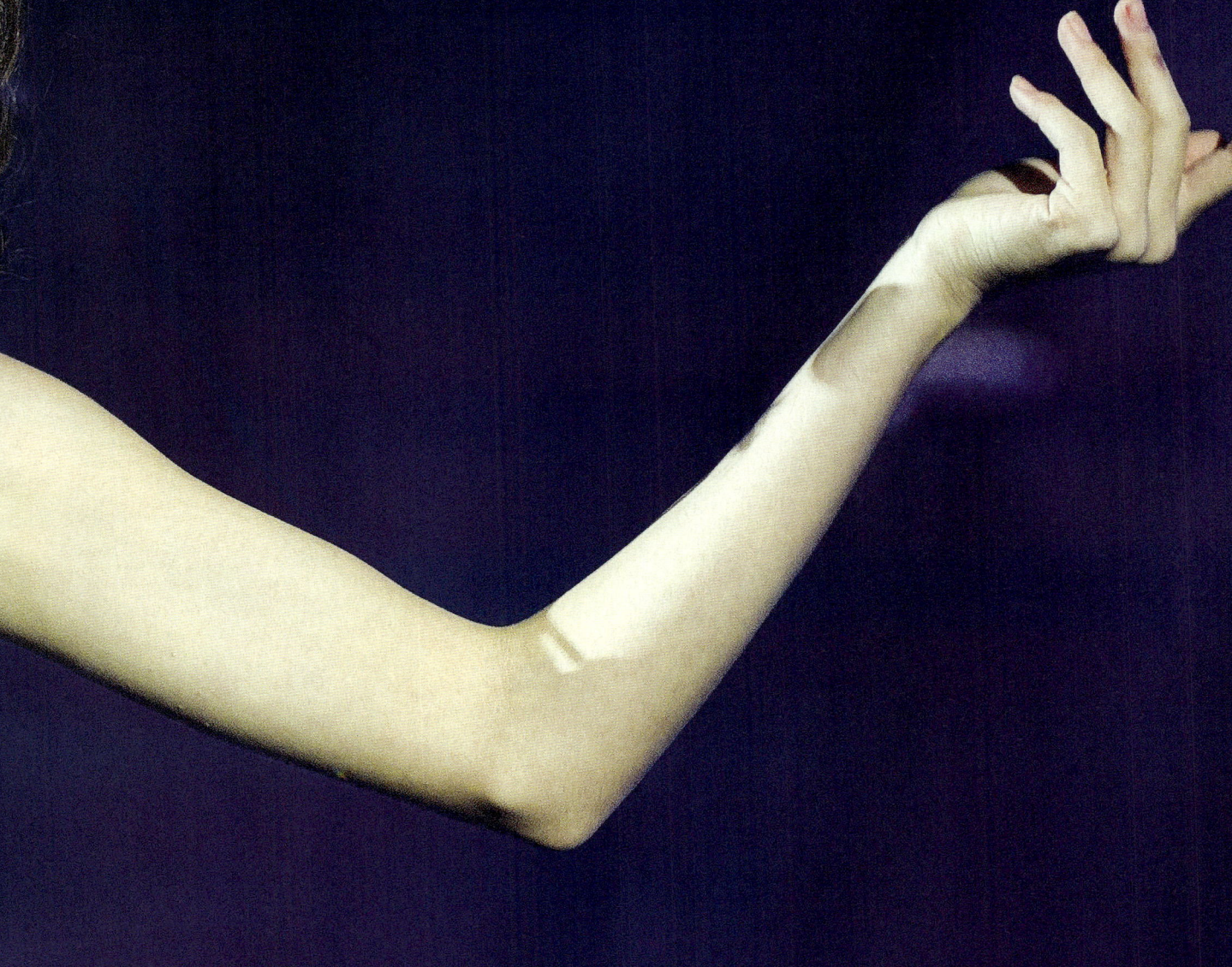

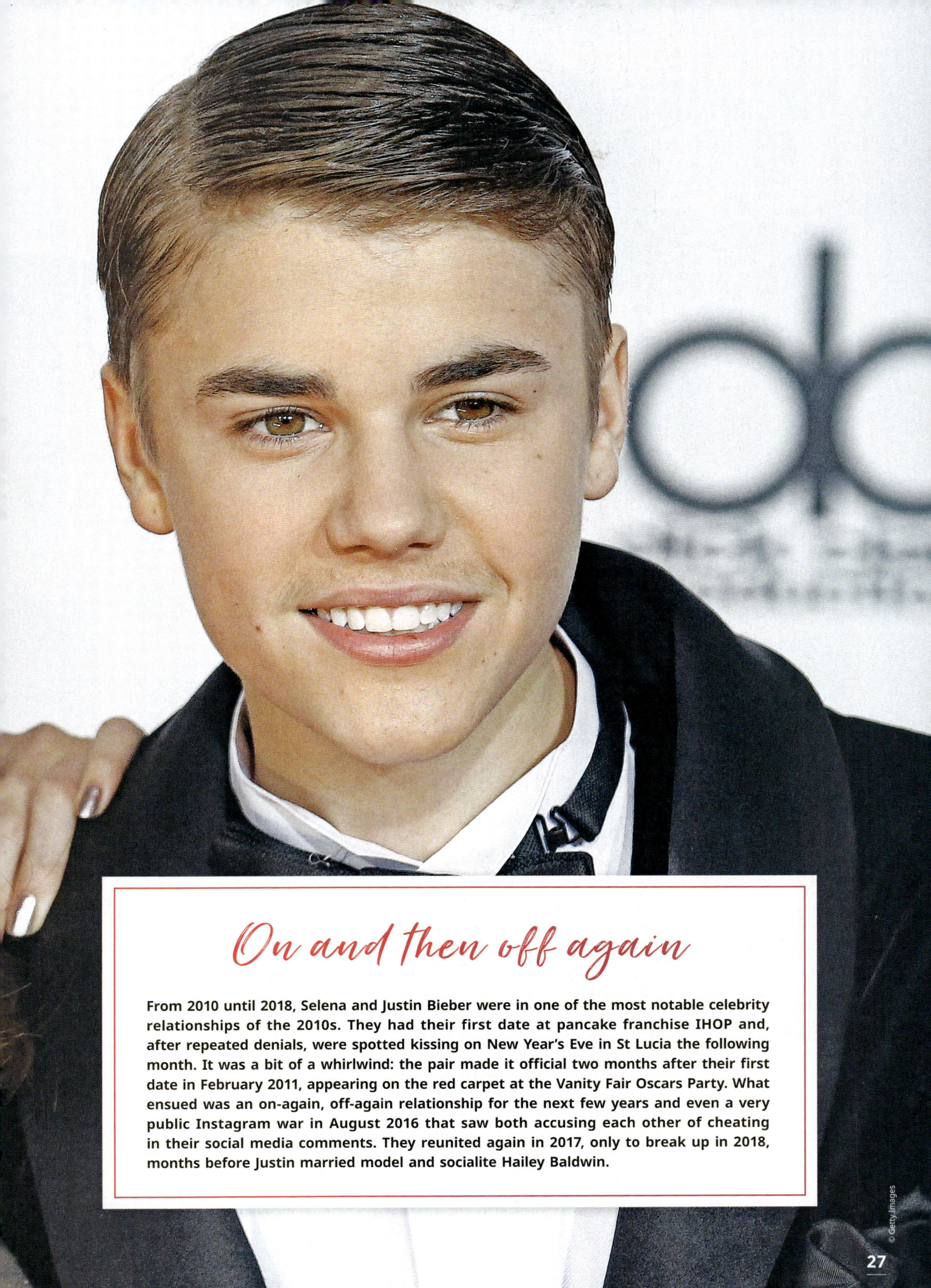

On and then off again

From 2010 until 2018, Selena and Justin Bieber were in one of the most notable celebrity relationships of the 2010s. They had their first date at pancake franchise IHOP and, after repeated denials, were spotted kissing on New Year's Eve in St Lucia the following month. It was a bit of a whirlwind: the pair made it official two months after their first date in February 2011, appearing on the red carpet at the Vanity Fair Oscars Party. What ensued was an on-again, off-again relationship for the next few years and even a very public Instagram war in August 2016 that saw both accusing each other of cheating in their social media comments. They reunited again in 2017, only to break up in 2018, months before Justin married model and socialite Hailey Baldwin.

ULTIMATE FAN'S GUIDE TO *Selena Gomez*

When the Sun Goes Down

Released in June 2011, *When the Sun Goes Down* was Selena Gomez & The Scene's final, and most successful, studio album. Debuting at number four in the US, the album's lead single, 'Who Says', became the band's most successful single, peaking at number 21 in the US charts, and their second single, 'Love You Like A Love Song' reached the top ten in Canada. In fact, 'Love You Like A Love Song' remains one of Selena's most popular songs. Critics gave mixed reviews of the track, with John Bergstrom of *PopMatters* referring to it as "credible, catchy and even sultry", but adding "it's all undone by a stuttering, Max Headroom non-chorus". Years after its release, *Pitchfork* would call it "a cult karaoke classic".

ULTIMATE FAN'S GUIDE TO *Selena Gomez*

Award-winning Wizards and an end to an era

Wizards of Waverly Place won an Emmy Award for Outstanding Children's Program in 2012. This year also saw the show coming to an end after four seasons. Selena herself won the Kids' Choice Award for Favourite Female TV Star five years in a row, celebrating the joy she brought to the screen. The show was praised for its sarcastic humour, alongside slapstick, situational comedy, which set it apart from other Disney Channel shows at the time. The show coming to an end allowed Selena to explore more mature roles. Despite ending, the show was extremely popular, so the cast returned for a television special – *The Wizards Return: Alex vs Alex* – in 2013.

ULTIMATE FAN'S GUIDE TO *Selena Gomez*

A loyal fan base

Selena's fiercely loyal fans are referred to as 'Selenators'. In 2014, Selena released items from her Dream Out Loud clothing line with 'Selenators' emblazoned on them, in an effort to acknowledge her fan base. The following year, Billboard asked fans to write about what being part of a fandom is like, with one passionate Selenator describing the community as "a family", writing "the bond that we share with Selena is something indescribable, unique and beautiful, and the love that we share has no limits, no end and it has something that no other fandom can ever compare to".

ULTIMATE FAN'S GUIDE TO *Selena Gomez*

Spring Breakers

In a departure from her more wholesome, family-friendly roles, Selena starred in the 2012 comedy crime film *Spring Breakers*. Directed by Harmony Korine (*Kids*, *Gummo*), the film follows a group of young women who go on spring break in Florida and meet a local drug dealer, played by James Franco, with whom they embark on a crime spree, testing the limits of their morality. The film received positive reviews of Selena's first mature role, with one review in the *New York Times* commenting on Selena's ability to engage in "behavior that feeds the tabloids without the humiliations and career-crushing price paid".

ULTIMATE FAN'S GUIDE TO *Selena Gomez*

Becoming Mavis Dracula

Selena starred in three of the *Hotel Transylvania* movies from 2012-22. She provided the voice for one of the main characters, Mavis Dracula, the daughter of Count Dracula and Martha. The franchise follows the monsters who live in the hotel and their adventures, with Count Dracula voiced by Adam Sandler, and Andy Samberg providing the voice for Mavis's love interest, Johnny. The first film was released to mixed reviews but was a box-office success, grossing $358.4 million against a budget of $85 million. The sequel, *Hotel Transylvania 2*, received more favourable reviews and grossed $474.8 million worldwide. Selena returned for the final instalment, *Hotel Transylvania: Transformania* in 2022, as both Mavis and as an executive producer.

ULTIMATE FAN'S GUIDE TO *Selena Gomez*

Stars Dance

More than a year after Selena announced she was taking a break from music, she released her debut solo studio album, *Stars Dance*, in July 2013. The album marked a more mature step for Selena and a more EDM and electropop sound. It also debuted at number one on the Billboard 200 and reached number one in Canada. Lead single, 'Come & Get It', really emulated those more mature themes, and the track was in the top ten in Canada, Ireland and the UK. The album was praised by critics for showing Selena's evolution as an artist, but some thought that there was an overuse of EDM production.

ULTIMATE FAN'S GUIDE TO *Selena Gomez*

Stars Dance Tour

Selena's first solo concert tour began in August 2013, spanning 55 shows in three continents: North America, Europe and Asia. The tour included performances of tracks from her solo debut album, *Stars Dance*, and releases with her band, Selena Gomez & The Scene. Selena was inspired by the performances of Britney Spears and Janet Jackson, and told reporters she "missed shows when it used to just be about the dancing and the performing as opposed to how big and elaborate the stage is so I kind of want to get back to that". The tour grossed $35.3 million but Selena was forced to cancel performances in Asia and Australia when she was diagnosed with lupus.

ULTIMATE FAN'S GUIDE TO *Selena Gomez*

Dealing with health issues

Selena was diagnosed with the chronic autoimmune disease lupus in 2014, confirming the diagnosis in 2015. To ease her symptoms, Selena cancelled shows for her Stars Dance Tour and went to rehab to receive chemotherapy. Then in 2016, she had to cancel some dates for her Revival Tour in Europe and South America due to the impact of her lupus diagnosis on her mental health. Selena has been subjected to trolls body shaming her and in early 2023, she took to TikTok to push back against the comments, telling followers that her medication causes her to hold "a lot of water weight", adding "I would much rather be healthy and take care of myself" and "my medications are important, and I believe that they're what helps me".

ULTIMATE FAN'S GUIDE TO *Selena Gomez*

"Disney's Teen Idol" no more

Selena decided to move from having her mother and stepfather as her managers in April 2014, signing with talent agencies WMA and Brillstein instead. The departure meant Selena could begin to break away from the image she had cultivated as a Disney Channel star, with *The Hollywood Reporter* suggesting "Selena's desire to find fresh handlers is part of a strategy to 'move into more adult-oriented fare in film and music'". Many Disney Channel stars have had to make the same transition, and Selena's came as no surprise after her role in *Spring Breakers* and her debut studio album.

For You

To complete her contract with Hollywood Records, Selena released her single 'The Heart Wants What It Wants' and her compilation album, *For You*, in 2014, which featured her greatest hits as well as three new tracks. The album debuted at number 24 on the Billboard 200, and 'The Heart Wants What It Wants', the only single released from the album, became her second top-ten hit in the US, reaching number six on the Billboard Hot 100. On the album, Selena commented, "I love my music so much and that's the idea of this album... kind of collecting the past four years and my favourite songs that I've been able to do from when I was 15 to now being 22".

ULTIMATE FAN'S GUIDE TO *Selena Gomez*

Taylena

Selena met Taylor Swift when they were both dating Jonas Brothers, Nick and Joe. The relationships ended but the love between friends strengthened. 'Taylena' are always cheering each other on and celebrating milestones, recently with Selena attending Taylor's inner circle 34th birthday party in New York. Selena appeared in Taylor's 'Bad Blood' music video as the villain, Arsyn. Selena shared with MTV News that the final showdown in the video was filled with love. "And I was like, 'I love you,' and she was like, 'I love you, too, and then we just slap each other. It was fun."

ULTIMATE FAN'S GUIDE TO *Selena Gomez*

Musical evolution

Selena began working on her second studio album and released the single 'I Want You To Know' with German producer and DJ, Zedd, in February 2015. 'I Want You To Know' was certified platinum in the US and Sweden, and was featured in several video games, including Guitar Hero Live. Shortly after recording the track, the pair began dating but broke up later that year. In June 2015, Selena released 'Good For You' in collaboration with rapper A$AP Rocky, serving as the lead single from her second studio album, *Revival*. This confident, sultry track continued the more mature trajectory of Selena's music career.

ULTIMATE FAN'S GUIDE TO *Selena Gomez*

Reinventing her music

Selena signed a new recording contract with Interscope Records in December 2014, soon after parting ways with Hollywood Records. A new recording contract brought with it the chance to reinvent her music, resulting in Selena's second studio album, *Revival*, which incorporated electropop and R&B. The album received more positive reviews from critics than her debut, and the album entered the US Billboard 200 at the number one spot, achieving Selena's highest first-week sales of her career. Selena cited Christina Aguilera as the album's major influence, and she collaborated with some huge industry names: Sia, Rock Mafia and Dreamlab, to name but a few.

ULTIMATE FAN'S GUIDE TO *Selena Gomez*

Expanding her filmography

Between 2015 and 2016, Selena quickly became a household name in the world of film. She made a cameo appearance in the 2015 financial comedy-drama *The Big Short*, and then as Dot in *The Fundamentals of Caring*, opposite Paul Rudd. Selena later appeared in *Neighbours 2: Sorority Rising* alongside a star-studded cast including fellow former Disney Channel star Zac Efron, as well as Seth Rogen and Rose Byrne. Selena was taking on more roles in films catered to an adult audience and continued to chip away at her Disney Channel persona, heralding a shift in her acting career.

Revival Tour

Selena's Revival Tour began in May 2016 and featured songs from her second solo studio album, *Revival*. The tour's first show was in Las Vegas, and she played shows in venues across North America, Asia, Australia and New Zealand. The Revival Tour featured an impressive roster of opening acts, including DNCE, Bea Miller and Charlie Puth, and Selena remarked that she was eager for it to focus more on her as an artist, with fewer effects. The tour was yet another success, grossing $35.6 million, but unfortunately, Selena had to cancel shows due to the impact of lupus on her health.

ULTIMATE FAN'S GUIDE TO *Selena Gomez*

'We Don't Talk Anymore'

In May 2016, Selena featured on Charlie Puth's hugely successful single 'We Don't Talk Anymore', taken from his debut studio album *Nine Track Mind*. The song is about the aftermath of a breakup, and it reached the top ten in multiple countries including the US, Australia and Spain. In fact, it was so successful that it was certified five times platinum, and the music video has garnered more than three billion views on YouTube, despite not actually featuring Selena. The track was also nominated for Best Collaboration at the 2017 MTV Video Music Awards, but lost to Zayn and Taylor Swift.

ULTIMATE FAN'S GUIDE TO *Selena Gomez*

Selena's global social media domination

Selena is a major global superstar and has a social media following worthy of one, too. At various points, she has been the most followed woman on Instagram, and in 2016 she became the first person to reach 100 million followers. Interestingly, this was also at a time when she had been less visible and engaged on social media, choosing to focus on her mental health, which she has frequently spoken about publicly. Social media is also a source of revenue for her: since 2017, she has been one of the top five highest-paid people on Instagram. In 2023, she became the most-followed woman on Instagram and has continued to be so as of 2024.

ULTIMATE FAN'S GUIDE TO *Selena Gomez*

Forbes 30 Under 30

Any musician who is influential enough to get their name into *Forbes* magazine's 30 Under 30 list is, by any definition, a big deal. The renowned business publication knows its stuff when it comes to honouring young people, so when Selena made the cut in 2016 and again four years later, her profile as a business operator and brand increased significantly. Aged 24 and 28 when *Forbes* included her in its list, Selena earned her spot both times through her entrepreneurial activities, her wide business interests, her ability to shine in many artistic fields – and of course, because of her $100m-plus fortune.

ULTIMATE FAN'S GUIDE TO *Selena Gomez*

Relationship with The Weeknd

In early January 2017, celeb websites went into overdrive with reports that Selena had been seen having dinner in Los Angeles with the songwriter Abel Tesfaye, who you know better as The Weeknd. Romance was definitely in the air, as the two were seen enjoying a smooch: not long afterwards, the couple were travelling to Italy and attending the Met Gala together. Social media posts from the two lovers soon made the relationship official, and the resulting gossip avalanche nearly broke the internet. Sadly, it was all over by 30 October, when a 'source' told *People* magazine: "It's been hard with him being on tour and her shooting in New York. That wasn't easy on them."

ULTIMATE FAN'S GUIDE TO *Selena Gomez*

'It Ain't Me' with DJ Kygo

'It Ain't Me' was a huge and incredibly catchy hit for Selena in the spring and summer of 2017. One listen to it and you'll see why: the sunny beats, the liquid vocals and the super-earworm falsetto chorus combine to make it a slab of perfect pop. A collaboration between Selena and the Norwegian DJ, Kygo, the song was a top ten in 27 countries, dominating nightclub playlists worldwide. The song is about a relationship that went south due to alcohol addiction, a depressing subject that contrasts neatly with its upbeat sound.

ULTIMATE FAN'S GUIDE TO *Selena Gomez*

Executive-producing 13 Reasons Why

Jay Asher's 2007 novel, *Thirteen Reasons Why*, dealt with the tricky subject of teenage suicide, meaning that any screen adaptation would need to be sensitively handled. When Selena was connected with the slightly-retitled TV version in 2017, first as a lead actor but then in the less public – but much more accountable – position of executive producer, she was obliged to handle controversies as they came up, and come up they soon did. "What Jay Asher created was a beautifully tragic, complicated yet suspenseful story," she said when talking about the Netflix show. "We wanted to do it justice, and yeah, the backlash is gonna come no matter what. It's not an easy subject to talk about."

ULTIMATE FAN'S GUIDE TO *Selena Gomez*

New tunes for 2017: 'Bad Liar', 'Fetish' and 'Wolves'

Turns out 2017 continued to be The Year Of Gomez, with three new singles – 'Bad Liar' (released on 18 May), 'Fetish' (13 July) and 'Wolves' (25 October). The first of these was a bass-driven dance floor anthem and came with a phone-friendly vertical music video that was the first to debut on Spotify. The second was a trancey, widescreen epic, featuring the rapper Gucci Mane, and appealed to fans of synth-heavy soundscapes. As for 'Wolves', this guitar-led singalong was a hit in several countries, but its bigger message was that the small matter of major surgery doesn't have to impact on artistic success, as we're about to discover...

Going public with her kidney transplant

Lupus, a chronic illness that can lead to serious health issues, is no joke – and when Selena revealed in 2015 that she had the disease, fans were justifiably sympathetic. In her case the condition required surgery in 2017, as she explained on social media. "I'm very aware some of my fans had noticed I was laying low for part of the summer and questioning why I wasn't promoting my new music, which I was extremely proud of," she wrote, adding "I found out I needed to get a kidney transplant due to my lupus and was recovering". Fortunately, the surgery went well, although an artery broke during the procedure and required attention. Selena's replacement kidney was donated by her friend, the actor Francia Raisa. "She gave me the ultimate gift and sacrifice by donating her kidney to me," Selena said. "I am incredibly blessed. I love you so much sis."

ULTIMATE FAN'S GUIDE TO *Selena Gomez*

Named Billboard's Woman of the Year

The Billboard magazine and website – and extended brand – is America's most prestigious metric for performance in music (as well as the RIAA's platinum, gold and silver certifications), so to be recognised in its annual Women In Music event is a significant honour. In recognition of Selena's commercial impact up to and including 2017, as well as her tireless activism and awareness-raising, she became that year's Woman Of The Year. "I've never felt this proud to be a woman in the industry than I do today, and that's because I actually feel comfortable with every single woman that has encouraged me," she said in her acceptance speech, thanking the women who came before her for "inspiring so many girls who don't feel that they have a voice".

ULTIMATE FAN'S GUIDE TO *Selena Gomez*

Brand ambassadorships for Puma, Coach and more

When you have a face and brand as recognisable as Selena's, companies waste no time pleading for your endorsement – and why not? Just some of the well-known corporations who have teamed up with Brand Gomez over the years include Adidas (2013), Pantene (2015), Louis Vuitton (2016), Coca-Cola (2016), Coach (2016) and PUMA (2017). Of the products that resulted, we reckon the coolest are Coach's limited-edition 'Selena Grace' range of handbags, and a ready-to-wear collection of clothes, bags and accessories named Coach X Selena Gomez. We also recommend PUMA's Phenom Lux sneakers and its SG x PUMA Strong Girl collection for the fashion-aware Gomez fan about town.

ULTIMATE FAN'S GUIDE TO *Selena Gomez*

Breaking records with Cardi B and friends

On 28 September 2018, Selena released the Spanish-language single 'Taki Taki' in collaboration with Cardi B, Ozuna and DJ Snake – and took another step towards superstardom in doing so. This song was the latest in no fewer than 16 consecutive top 40 hits on the Billboard Hot 100, and if that wasn't enough, later in 2018 Selena was named as Spotify's most-streamed artist. Only a very small number of musicians were now operating at her commercial level, her friend Taylor Swift and her former beau The Weeknd arguably among them. What was next for Selena to conquer?

ULTIMATE FAN'S GUIDE TO *Selena Gomez*

All over the screen in '19

As if Selena wasn't busy enough, you might have seen her acting in a couple of interesting film roles in 2019. The first, *The Dead Don't Die*, was a surreal zombie movie directed by the auteur Jim Jarmusch and featured a stellar cast of actors such as Steve Buscemi; the second, *A Rainy Day in New York*, was a decent film but suffered from limited distribution due to the unsavoury accusations levelled that year at its director, Woody Allen. Selena also acted as an executive producer for a Netflix documentary called *Living Undocumented*, devoted to the subject of immigrant families in the USA: she explained that the issue appealed to her because of her own family history.

A NETFLIX ORIGINAL DOCUMENTARY SERIES

LIVING | UNDOCUMENTED

FROM EXECUTIVE PRODUCER SELENA GOMEZ

BEHIND
EVERY
AMERICAN
STORY

IS THE
FIGHT
FOR
FREEDOM

OCTOBER 2 | NETFLIX

ULTIMATE FAN'S GUIDE TO *Selena Gomez*

'Lose You To Love Me'

Kicking off the *Rare* album campaign in fine style in the autumn of 2019, Selena released 'Lose You To Love Me', a confessional song that addressed the end of her relationship with Justin Bieber. It came with a black-and-white video – shot entirely on an iPhone – and was inescapable through the winter and into 2020, or better known as the first year of the COVID-19 pandemic. The song was a massive hit, occupying the top ten of the charts in several countries and scoring multi-platinum certifications around the world. The Gomez fanbase was clearly willing to jump on board the *Rare* era of Selena's career – and they weren't about to be put off by some pesky virus.

ULTIMATE FAN'S GUIDE TO *Selena Gomez*

Rare

The sound of modern pop has been shaped in recent years by a handful of strong, commercial albums, most of which use multiple approaches to get their message across. *Rare*, **Selena's album released on 10 January 2020, is one of those key releases, covering sounds such as R&B, reggaeton and funk. Danceable, relatable and thoughtful, the songs cover a gamut of vibes, from joy to introspection and back, and millions of fans snapped up the album. Like its two predecessors,** *Rare* **debuted at the top of the Billboard 200 chart, and accumulated almost 80 million streams for its tracks in its first week: you could reasonably say that it was a success…**

Placing mental health front and centre

Aside from her entertainment career, Selena is known for her philanthropy work and in particular, her advocacy for mental health awareness. For years, she has used her platform to de-stigmatise mental health and she has long been vocal about her experiences with it, hoping that this will help others get the support they need. In April 2020, Selena publically revealed that she had been diagnosed with bipolar disorder after she had checked into a mental health facility in 2018, during which time she took one of her several breaks from social media. Selena would later discuss her journey with bipolar disorder in the 2022 documentary *My Mind & Me*, directed by Alek Keshishian.

ULTIMATE FAN'S GUIDE TO *Selena Gomez*

Giving back through activism

A full list of Selena's awareness- and fund-raising activities for various causes would require this entire publication, so let's just list a few. From 2009, she worked on behalf of the charities Island Dog and Raise Hope For Congo; she promoted climate-change awareness through Disney's Friends For Change; she appeared at the Children's Hospital of Philadelphia; and she narrated *Girl Rising*, a 2013 documentary about education. Selena has also assisted the WE Day 2019 and WE Charity efforts, donated $3 million to fight Australian wildfires, advocated for the LGBTQ+ community in several fundraising projects and spoken out on pro-choice issues. She has been vocal as a COVID-19 vaccine supporter, supported the Black Lives Matter movement, and even hosted a Mental Health Youth Action Forum event at the White House in 2022.

ULTIMATE FAN'S GUIDE TO *Selena Gomez*

Cooking up a storm on TV

Hungry? Watch *Selena + Chef*, the HBO Max cooking show that takes us inside Selena's kitchen for a weekly look at her culinary skills. Premiering on 13 August 2020 – coincidentally, the same month that she collaborated with K-Pop band BLACKPINK on a song called 'Ice Cream' – the show features our heroine plus a professional guest chef, cooking up a storm and raising money for the charity of the guest's choice. Over four seasons, as well as 2023's holiday special, *Selena + Chef: Home For The Holidays*, we've witnessed Selena and her guests coming up with all sorts of delectable recipes, offering tips and advice for budding chefs and talking about causes close to their hearts. With a fifth season greenlit for 2024, we won't be tuning out any time soon.

Beauty and the brand

In September 2020, Selena founded a charity called the Rare Impact Fund, whose stated goal is to raise $100 million over a decade for global mental health services and education for young people. That's a vast sum of money by any standards, but the Fund is supported by a percentage of sales from Selena's Rare Beauty cosmetics line. There is a wealth of cool stuff to choose from in the Rare Beauty catalogue – the original line included 48 shades of foundation, matte lip creams, eyebrow definers, liquid blush, and lip balms – all packaged in recyclable, cruelty-free, vegan materials certified by the Forest Stewardship Council. If you would like to contribute, Rare Beauty products are available through the Space.NK chain in the UK and Sephora in the US.

ULTIMATE FAN'S GUIDE TO *Selena Gomez*

Revelación

Paying homage to her heritage, Selena released a Spanish-language EP called *Revelación* in March 2021: fans and critics were delighted with the project, labelling it a logical move for her to make at this point in her career. Its sound is a combination of reggaeton, Urbano and Latin-flavoured R&B, a mixture that took it to the top of Billboard's Top Latin Albums chart and gave it 8.57 million streams on Spotify in its first 24 hours. *Revelación* was nominated for Best Latin Pop Album at the Grammy Awards in 2022, as well as receiving Latin Pop Album Of The Year nominations from the Billboard Latin Music, Latin American Music and Lo Nuestro awarding organisations. At this point in her career, it seemed as though Selena could do no wrong.

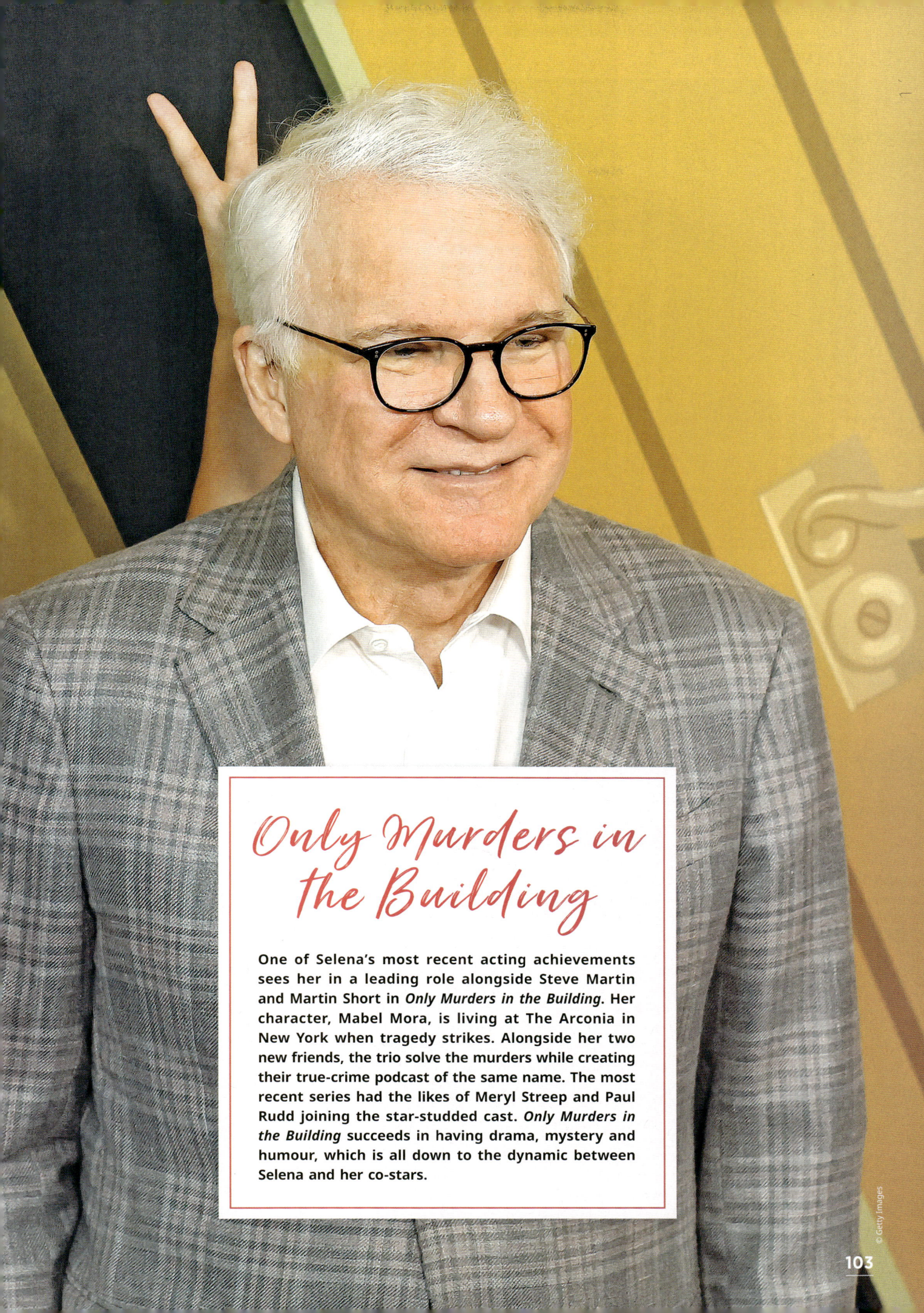

Only Murders in the Building

One of Selena's most recent acting achievements sees her in a leading role alongside Steve Martin and Martin Short in *Only Murders in the Building*. Her character, Mabel Mora, is living at The Arconia in New York when tragedy strikes. Alongside her two new friends, the trio solve the murders while creating their true-crime podcast of the same name. The most recent series had the likes of Meryl Streep and Paul Rudd joining the star-studded cast. *Only Murders in the Building* succeeds in having drama, mystery and humour, which is all down to the dynamic between Selena and her co-stars.

ULTIMATE FAN'S GUIDE TO *Selena Gomez*

'Calm Down' remix with Rema

The Nigerian singer Divine Ikubor, better known as Rema, enjoyed a major UK and European hit in February 2022 with his song 'Calm Down' – and when his label, Interscope, decided to remix the track for potential American success, who better to ask for a guest vocal than Selena? Released in the summer of '22, 'Calm Down (Remix)' was a mid-tempo banger that lit up dancefloors from Miami to Los Angeles – but more importantly, it gave the Afrobeat genre a major boost in visibility in North America. Rema himself labels his sound 'Afro-rave', which perfectly sums up its uptempo, beats-heavy vibe, so if you're in a party mood, we suggest that you fire it up immediately.

ULTIMATE FAN'S GUIDE TO *Selena Gomez*

Impact of Selena Gomez: My Mind & Me

In 2022, Selena allowed us a closer look into her life behind the camera with her documentary *Selena Gomez: My Mind & Me*. The documentary covers six years of her life following her struggles with physical and mental illness, where she explores the impact of living with lupus and bipolar disorder. Selena has been praised for her raw, intimate account of experiencing these difficulties, which helps to break the stigma around physical and mental health. In the documentary, she mentions "what makes me happy is connection and it helps me get out of my head". Wise words we could all live by.

ULTIMATE FAN'S GUIDE TO *Selena Gomez*

Gomez versus Bieber: how it went down

In 2023, a supposed feud sprang up between Selena and Hailey Bieber, the wife of her ex, Justin Bieber, although there was very little substance to it, with the online commentary from overexcited followers of both celebs making a mountain out of a molehill. It began when Hailey posted a TikTok of herself and chums singing "I'm not saying she deserved it, but God's timing is always right", which was interpreted as a dig at Selena, as it happened after some tabloids commented on Selena's weight. All credit to Selena, who wrote "It's OK! I don't let these things get me down! Be nice to everyone!" Hailey backed off, claiming, "We were just having a girls' night and did a random TikTok sound for fun. It's not directed at anyone." Using the opportunity for a teachable moment, Selena then added: "Hailey Bieber reached out to me and let me know that she has been receiving death threats and such hateful negativity... This isn't what I stand for. No-one should have to experience hate or bullying. I've always advocated for kindness and really want this to all stop."

ULTIMATE FAN'S GUIDE TO *Selena Gomez*

Romance with Benny Blanco

On 8 December 2023, an Instagram fan account posted a picture of Selena getting chummy with the producer Benny Blanco, to which she responded: "He is my absolute everything in my heart". When it was pointed out that Blanco had allegedly said something mean about Selena in 2020 ("Justin Bieber is not one of those, like, cookie-cutter pop artists, you know they're, like, 'This is my new single and here's my makeup line'"), she replied "Lol yeah and he's still better than anyone I've ever been with. Facts." The online trolls swarmed on this, of course, and – perhaps oddly for someone in her position – she engaged with them directly, telling one poster who disapproved of Selena-plus-Benny: "He's been the best thing that's ever happened to me. The end."

ULTIMATE FAN'S GUIDE TO *Selena Gomez*

A busy year ahead

Selena has a lot of exciting projects lined up for 2024. Her highly anticipated album comeback, which comes four years after the release of her last album *Rare*, is expected to be released soon. However, this could potentially be her last album, as she mentioned on the *SmartLess* podcast that she wants to focus on her acting career: "I do feel like I have one more album in me, but I would probably choose acting". In other exciting news, she has recently confirmed that *Wizards of Waverly Place* will be returning with a sequel, and she will serve as executive producer for the project alongside her on-screen brother, David Henrie. With so much to look forward to, Selena fans better watch this space…